BONSAI

BONSAI

CHARTWELL
BOOKS, INC.

Published by Chartwell Books
A Division of Book Sales Inc.
114 Northfield Avenue
Edison, New Jersey 08837
USA

ISBN 0-7858-0974-0

This book is produced by
Quantum Books Ltd
6 Blundell Street
London N7 9BH

Project Manager: Rebecca Kingsley
Project Editor: Judith Millidge
Design/Editorial: David Manson
Andy McColm, Maggie Manson

The material in this publication previously appeared in
Bonsai: The Art of Growing and Keeping Miniature Trees,
Bonsai Identifier

QUMSPBN
Set in Futura
Reproduced in Singapore by Eray Scan
Printed in Singapore by Star Standard Industries (Pte) Ltd

Contents

THE LIVING ART OF BONSAI

Bonsai is often referred to as the Japanese art of miniature trees. Its origins, however are in China. The word bonsai comes from the Chinese words *pun-sai*. It was the Chinese who developed many of the creative techniques and then exported them to Japan nearly 500 years ago.

The Meaning of Bonsai

Literally translated, the Chinese words *pun-sai* (with the emphasis on *'sai'* as in 'sighing') mean 'tree in a pot'. However, merely having a potted tree does not necessarily make it a bonsai.

BONSAI DEFINED

A bonsai is an artistic replica of a natural tree in miniature form. It consists of two elements: the living tree and the container. The two elements have to be in harmony and the selection of the right pot for a tree is almost an art form in itself.

The plant may be a vine, shrub or a tree, but is commonly referred to as simply a tree. The container is usually a conventional pot or slab of interesting rock. A bonsai is never called a 'bonsai tree'. The word already includes the living element. Once out of a pot, the tree ceases to be a bonsai.

Left. Pyracantha angustifolia.
Age approximately 70 years.

*Above. Common Hawthorn, in the literati
style. Age 50 years. Span 17in.*

ANCIENT BONSAI

It is important to understand that a bonsai is not just any miniature tree growing in any container. In Japan, top-quality bonsai are several hundred years old and are truly living works of art. They have been carefully attended over the years and handed down through generations from father to son. Most Western bonsai will only ever be shadows of the form and spirit of these ancient Japanese masterpieces.

THE ILLUSION OF AGE

Age is a factor in bonsai, but it is not important in itself. Being old does not necessarily mean that it will be a better bonsai than one that is much younger. What is important are the characteristics of age. While much can be done to enhance the illusion of age, true age is accompanied by the formation of mature bark and solid trunks. In very old species, the bark may be deeply furrowed by as much as 2in.

Outdoor and Indoor Bonsai

Many people are surprised to learn that most bonsai spend all of their time outdoors. They may think that bonsai are delicate and need the protection of an indoor environment — nothing could be further from the truth.

OUTDOOR BONSAI

Some trees may indeed be over-wintered indoors in an unheated room or greenhouse, but many will be left outdoors all the time, perhaps with only an occasional watering so that they do not dry out. During particularly cold winters, some species will need to be moved indoors or sheltered outside, as a bonsai is generally not as hardy as the same species growing in the ground. This is because when growing naturally, the plant's roots descend a long way into the earth, and unless frost penetrates particularly deeply, the roots are not usually affected by it. However, in a small amount of soil, roots are more vulnerable to frost and require to be protected

Left. Serissa foetida, *Tree of a Thousand Stars, in a Chinese group arrangement.*

Above. Podocarpos macrophyllus.

INDOOR BONSAI

There are those species, of course, that make what are called indoor bonsai, for which there is a very considerable demand. Despite their popularity they can be quite difficult to maintain, and many trees are lost through lack of understanding of their general horticultural needs. Many indoor bonsai are treated as house plants, and fed and watered like house plants, when they should really be treated like trees.

The species used for indoor bonsai are usually subtropical or tropical plants, and while they like being outdoors in the summer, they need to be kept well above freezing all year. Some demand high room temperatures during the day and night, making them quite difficult to care for.

Remember! Each bonsai is an individual. Refer to the entries in the directory section (see p.16) for specific guidance.

Bonsai Shapes and Styles

For many years, bonsai has been recognized as an art form in Japan. Unfortunately, such recognition in the West is a long way off, due to lack of tradition and the need for new caretakers to maintain and develop the trees after the previous owner's death.

A LIVING 'CANVAS'

Once set, the shape needs to be maintained, and the design changed from time to time, as one part develops more than another, or as the grower sees the tree in a different light. The design is never really finished. New growth provides an ever-changing canvas on which to 'paint' the bonsai.

INFINITE BONSAI

Look at a few different trees that are growing naturally and you will see an infinite variety of shapes. Some grow singly, some in small groups, others in large forests. Some have more than one trunk, and others have been blown down and have rerooted themselves at a strange angle. Bonsai reflects all these natural arrangements.

*Left. Larch, grown in the wind-swept style.
Age about 50 years.*

*Above. Japanese White Pine.
Age 30 years. Rooted on rock.*

 BONSAI STYLES

1. SINGLE TRUNK		**2. MULTI-TRUNKED**	
Formal upright	Cascade	Twin trunk	Triple trunk
Informal upright	Semi-cascade	Multiple trunk	Root connected
Slanting	Weeping		
Wind-swept	Literati	**3. MULTI-TREE or GROUP**	
Split trunk	Exposed root	Group planting	
Driftwood	Root over rock	Planted on rock	
Broom	Planted on rock	Landscape	

Bonsai Size Classification

To the layman one bonsai is very much like another. To a connoisseur, however, every bonsai is quite different. Not only are there different styles of bonsai, but there are different sizes too.

BONSAI HEIGHTS

Bonsai range in size from 2in high to over 6ft. In Japan, trees over 4ft are not considered bonsai as the term describes miniature trees. In China potted trees are often grown well over 10ft tall. Classification of bonsai by size can only be arbitrary as there are no rules.

COMMON BONSAI SIZES

● up to 2in	Thimble
● 2–6in	*Mame**
● 6–12in	Small
● 12–24in	Medium
● 24–48in	Big
● 4ft	Very large

* pronounced marmay

Right. Dwarf Spruce, grown in the miniature Mame style. Height only 4in.

How to Use this Book

Throughout the directory section, key icons are used to provide the reader with a snapshot reference of the character and care required to cultivate bonsai.

PHYSICAL ATTRIBUTES

The members of certain genera have species that are either trees or shrubs. Some species are evergreen and some are deciduous. A bonsai is denoted as flowering, fruiting or coning only when these are significant features. All these characteristics are shown below.

CARE AND ATTENTION

The more difficult a bonsai is to cultivate the more care is required to be successful. In the yellow boxes throughout the directory, we have indicated how much care is needed by each bonsai with 4 being the greatest amount and 1 being the least.

Tree		**Flowering**	
Shrub		**Fruiting**	
Evergreen		**Coning**	
Deciduous		**Care**	

BONSAI SPECIES

Bonsai knows no barriers of race, culture, religion or even class. It has a following in every country today and attracts people from every stratum of society. Bonsai has a unifying influence on people and is continuously increasing in popularity throughout the world.

The following directory includes the main bonsai subjects likely to be encountered, but is by no means all-inclusive.

ABIES SPP. FIR

Not all conifers are firs. Genuine firs are easily distinguished from trees with simliar foliage by the two prominent white bands, stomata, found on the back of the needles. Their branch arrangement is in whorls and the bark later forms blisters which carry resin. Few firs are used in the West for bonsai as the species available have needles that are too long and stiff to work with.

Style Formal, informal. literati, group plantings.
Characteristics Smooth bark which blisters later.
Color Bright green foliage with voilet/purple cones.
Care Sun protection is needed in summer with frequent misting. Its shape is maintained by pinching out the ends of new growth in the spring.

Above. Korean Fir in the twin tree style. Age 15 years. Height 14in.

ACER SPP. MAPLE

Maples are one of the top three subjects used for bonsai, along with pines and junipers. Most quality bonsai will be either Trident Maples (*A. buergeranum*), or Japanese Maples (*A. japonicum*, *A palmatum*). There is a variety of species and leaf shape, color and quality. They are frequently grown as small groups or forests, as well as growing their roots over a rock. Maples are grown almost exclusively as outdoor bonsai.

Style Formal, informal, cascading, literati, group, mame.
Characteristics Deciduous. Flowers are insignificant.
Color Early spring color and fiery, intense autumn tints.
Care Protect from winds. Midday sun should be avoided and ornamental varieties need winter protection. Repot every two to three years.

Above. Japanese Mountain Maple. Age 80 years. Height 31in.

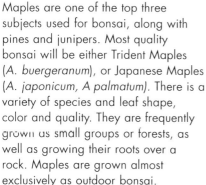

Above. *Acer palmatum linerlobum,* a variety of Japanese Mountain Maple.
Age 10 years. Height 20in.

BERBERIS SPP. BARBERRY

Barberry is not a classical bonsai subject even though it is of oriental origin. It is a shrub with small leaves. Some are deciduous, others evergreen, but the evergreens usually replace their leaves each year. Colored species, and those that make good autumn color, are used such as, Japanese Barberry (B. *Ihunbergii*). Some of these grow into very tall shrubs and have the potential to make good-quality bonsai with thick and solid trunks.

Above. Japanese Barberry.
Age 35 years. Height 18in.

Style Informal, multi-trunked, group plantings, mame.
Characteristics Small flowers, daisy-like and interesting colored fruit in the autumn.
Color Red or orange flowers early in the year.
Care Easy to care for. Until the roots are established do not repot it. Some winter protection is needed. When pruned, the stems and roots have an intense yellow inner color.

B E R B E R I S

BETULA SPP. BIRCH

B E T U L A

The Silver Birch is commonly planted in parks instead of the Common Birch, as it is a delicately foliaged small tree, with weeping branches and silvered bark that peels off, displaying a rich undercolor. The leaves are small making it an ideal subject for bonsai. They are deciduous but rarely make good autumn color. They are hardly ever pictured in Japanese books, although listed in catalogues of species suitable for bonsai.

Style Informal, cascading, literati, multi-trunked, mame.
Characteristics Silver colored bark. Graceful and elegant.
Color Red or orange flowers.
Care Full sun needed and watered well. They are very sturdy and have no other requirements.

Above. *Betulus verrucosa.*
Age 12 years. Height 20in.

BUXUS SPP. BOX

Box is a genus of usually small evergreen shubs, although some do reach tree-like proportions. Growth is stiff and angular so it is not easy to make acceptable-looking bonsai. Common Box (*B. semperivens*) is not too different from the Small-Leaved or Japanese Box (*B. microphylla*). Trees with a good glossy shine to the leaves are perhaps best, as they give the tree plenty of sparkle.

Style Informal, multi-trunked, literati, mame.
Characteristics Highly suitable for bonsai and easy to grow.
Color Small, green glossy foliage.
Care Needs to be protected from frosts in winter. Regular thinning out of foliage to maintain shape.

Above. *Buxus sinica.*
Age 80 years. Height 24in.

C A R P I N U S

CARPINUS SPP. HORNBEAM, IRONWOOD

Hornbeam is popular for bonsai, both in the West and Japan. It is not one of the easiest subjects, as it grows quickly and needs a lot of attention in the early days. Deciduous with leaves similar to beech, but narrower and more veined. In the West, the Common or European Hornbeam (*C. betuls*) will usually be used. Korean Hornbeam (*C. turczaninivii*) is a species with autumn colors but is not easy to come by in the West.

Style Formal, informal, cascading, multi-trunked, literati, group, mame.
Characteristics An elegant tree, fast growing and deciduous.
Color Silvery-purple colored fluting of the bark on the trunk.
Care The leaves burn when in full sun and wind. It does not like to be over-watered. Constant grooming is needed to maintain the shape.

Above. Japanese Hornbeam.
Age unknown – very old. Height 12in.

CEDRUS SPP. CEDAR

Cedars are often mistaken for larches, but their evergreen status distinguishes them. They have thinner stems when grown as bonsai than larches and the needle quality is different—those on cedar look stiff rather than soft. They are ideal for making into windswept trees and can be grown in a variety of styles. Often used for bonsai these days is *C. atlantica glauca*, the Blue Atlas Cedar, which is available in most garden centers.

Style Formal upright, informal, multi-trunked, groups.

Characteristics Short spurs of growth with weeping ends.

Color Blue-green needles with light green cones.

Care Fussy subjects, they need to be kept on the dry side. They do not like root pruning too often. Repotting can cause all the needles to drop, but a new flush quickly follows.

Above. Blue Atlas Cedar.
Age 20 years. Height 15in.

CHAENOMELES SPP. FLOWERING QUINCE

Flowering Quince make a lovely show of color during the early part of the year, depending on where the specimen is located. The flowers form before leaf break and continue for a long time. Commonly referred to as Japonica, they are a popular garden plant. Quality bonsai Flowering Quince have usually been dug up from gardens and potted up to make into bonsai.

Style Informal, cascading, literati, multi-trunked, mame.
Characteristics Massive, extensive stump with short flower bearing shoots.
Color Flowers are red or pink with yellow centers. Fruit when formed is yellow and large.
Care Feed to encourage flowering. After flowering, deadhead the tree and check that no fruit has formed to sap the tree's energy.

Above. Flowering Quince.
Age 5 years. Height 9in.

CHAMAECYPARIA SPP. FALSE CYPRESS

False Cypresses are evergreen conifers. As this species is readily available in garden centers, it is often used as bonsai, although it is only the Hinoki Cypress (*C. obtusa*) that really measures up to the standards for a quality bonsai. False Cypresses are often grouped together, making forests of upright trees. Other varieties used are Sawara Cypress (*C. pisifera*), and the cultivar *C. lawsoniana* 'Ellwoodii'.

Style Formal, informal, multi-trunked, groups, literati, mame.
Characteristics Compact, scale-like foliage.
Color Good, deep-green color.
Care This species demands a lot of attention, needing wind protection in winter, and shade in summer. New growth should be pinched out to prevent dense foliage developing.

Above. Sawara Cypress.
Age 10 years. Height 47in.

CORNUS SPP. DOGWOOD

Not all dogwoods have colored stems, it is mainly the shrubby ones from North America that are so colorful. European and Asian species tend to grow into small trees and make good bonsai specimens. Dogwoods are deciduous with veined leaves. Leaves and new shoots tend to be parallel to the stem on which they grow. In Japan, *C. kousa* is the main species used for bonsai.

Style Informal, cascading, mame, multi-trunked.
Characteristics Distinctively paired, veined leaves.
Color Flowers are red or pink with yellow centers. Fruit when formed is yellow and large.
Care Wind and sun protection is needed. Feed with care to control new growth.

Above. Cornelian Cherry. Age 16 years. Height 8in.

COTONEASTER SPP.

This small-leaved species make attractive bonsai. They are usually angular in growing habit and creep slowly. They are used extensively in Japan and in the West. The leaves of *C. horizontalis* turn beautiful shades of red and orange in the autumn before they fall. Small flowers come in spring, followed by red berries in the autumn. It is ideal for making into small-scale bonsai, called *mame*, and some are just a few inches high.

Above. *Cotoneaster horizontalis.*
Age 25 years. Height 10in.

Style Informal, cascading, mame, multi-trunked.
Characteristics Small leaves and angular in habit.
Color Red and orange leaves with red berries, in the autumn.
Care Easy to grow, needing no special care. Feed well. Most do not need winter protection.

COTONEASTER

CRATAEGUS SPP. HAWTHORN

Hawthorn is a small tree armed with thorns, not flowering until it is about 20 years old. It is renowned for its flowers, pure white to intense red in color. The bark is deeply furrowed and when grown in open spaces, naturally takes on an interesting shape. Growth is angular but a good bonsai must look like a miniature tree. Only a few of the species are commonly available.

Style Formal, informal, cascading.

Characteristics Flower quality, distinctive leaves which are often deeply incised.

Color Pure white to intense red flowers. The berries are usually red or orange.

Care Needs considerable care to contain growth and to guard against fungal and insect attack.

Above. Common Hawthorn. Age 16 years. Height 8in.

CRATAEGUS

30

CRYPTOMERIA SPP. JAPANESE CEDAR

Although not a member of the genus of trees, Cryptomeria is often called Japanese Cedar. It is used regularly for bonsai in Japan and China, where they make tall, narrow trees with a solid buttress base. The evergreen leaves are packed around the shoot which is not really visible. Cryptomeria only comes as the species *C. japonica*, but there are a host of cultivars, a few of which are better suited to bonsai than others.

Above. *Cryptomeria japonica yatsubusa.* Age 4–8 years. Height 28in.

Style Upright, sometimes in small groups or forest arrangements.
Characteristics Reddish-brown bark which peels off in long strips on the trunk.
Color Bright green-blue foliage in the growing season, turning reddish-brown for winter.
Care Pinching out new growth is needed to keep this species in good condition.

EHRETIA SPP.

This is a small genus of tropical tree that is also referred to as Carmona. They make small trees and either deciduous or evergreen, and form panicles of small white flowers in early summer. Evergreen forms are not usually hardy in the West and when used for bonsai are considered an indoor subject. Fulkien Tea (*E. buxifolia*), an evergreen with small box-like leaves, is used for making bonsai in China and Southeast Asia.

Above. *Ehretia buxofilia.*
Age 50 years. Height 45in.

Style Formal, informal including literati and groups.
Characteristics Crackled bark surface with age.
Color Light gray bark, white flowers in early summer.
Care Pinching back new shoots and misting using distilled water is needed regularly.

FAGUS SPP. BEECH

Beeches are classical bonsai subjects. They are well-suited for training into either formal, upright-style bonsai or less formal, with an asymmetric shape. The Common or European Beech (*F. sylvatica*) is used in the West; its equivalent in Japan is the White or Japanese Beech (*F. crenata*), named after the color of its trunk. *F. sylvatica*, green-leaved, and *F. sylvatica atropurpurea*, purple leaved, will frequently be found.

Above. *Fagus. sylvatica.*
Age 50 years. Height 26in.

Style Formal and informal.
Characteristics Occasional brilliant white bark on young trees.
Color Light gray bark, green or purple leaved.
Care Easy to grow. Defoliation has to take place immediately after new leaves have hardened. Aphids are attracted to beeches.

Figs used for bonsai come mainly from tropical and subtropical climes, and are treated as indoor bonsai. Some are deciduous, others are evergreen, and the fruit is not always edible. Aerial roots are made by some species and these are features in a bonsai. Aged specimens can be very expensive to acquire. The Weeping Fig, or Benjamin Tree *(F. benjamina)* is commonly available. Other species include *F. salicifolia* and *F. retusa*.

Style Informal, group plantings.
Characteristics Supple stems which allow it to be trained into many shapes.
Color Variegated or unvariegated leaved species.
Care Need to be kept away from draughts indoors. Provide a humid microclimate and spray plants daily with water.

Above. *Ficus retusa.*
Age 174 years. Height 33in.

GINKGO SPP.

Ginkgo is a deciduous tree in a group all of its own. Sometimes described as a conifer, it is not a conifer as such. It makes a narrow, upright tree that only in old age starts to spread and look old. There is only one species in this genus, with a few varieties which are rarely seen. The Ginkgo in the West is not suitable for bonsai as the leaf is of poor quality. The cultivar *G.biloba* 'Chichi Icho' is used in Japan.

Style Informal, group, multi-trunked,
Characteristics Either fan-shaped or deeply incised leaves.
Color Butter-yellow leaves or fruit may be displayed in the autumn.
Care Regular pruning to keep the shape compact.

Above. *Gingko biloba.*
Age 150 years. Height 32in.

JUNIPERUS SPP. JUNIPER

This is one of the top three species of tree used for bonsai, along with pine and maple. No bonsai collection is complete without a number of them and in a variety of styles. All the older bonsai in Japan have been collected from the wild and are at least 50 or 100 years or more old before being transferred to a pot. *J. chinensis sargentii* and Needle Juniper (*J.rigida*) are the classic subjects in Japan and the West.

Style Formal, informal, cascading, literati, multi-trunked, mame.
Characteristics Extremely hardy and long-lived.
Color Steely blue-green to light green with gold or silvery hues.
Care Regular pinching out is needed in the growing season and foliage thinned in the autumn to let in light.

Above. Chinese Juniper.
Age 70 years. Height 30in.

Above. *Juniperus chinensis 'Blaauw'.*
Age 10 years. Height 9in.

L A R I X

Larch is a deciduous conifer which is interesting in spring and autumn. Small, egg-shaped cones are long-lasting and in proportion to the tree. The flowers are elegant and significant in some species. Only a few species of larch used for bonsai, either the Japanese Larch (*L. leptolepsis*) or European Larch (*L. decidua*). In winter the Japanese Larch is reddish in appearance, and the European is yellow.

Above. Japanese Larch.
Age 50 years. Height 28in.

Style Formal or informal.
Characteristics Easy to obtain and the trunk thickens quickly.
Color In autumn foliage turns either a golden or a pinkish yellow before dropping.
Care Needs some shade in summer to prevent the leaves burning. Very hardy and resilient, needing no winter protection.

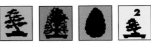

Above. European Larch group planting.
Age 30 years. Height 32in.

MALUS SPP. CRAB APPLE

Crab apples are one of the premier flowering species used for bonsai. There is quite a variation in flowering capacities and quality of fruit produced. In Japan, many bonsai created for export are propagated by air layering from a stock tree which has reached flowering maturity. Those likely to be encountered are Hall's Crab Apple (*M. halliana*), *M. sieboldii*, Toringo Crab Apple (*M. toringoides*) and *M. cerasifera*.

Above. *Mallus halliana*.
Age 30 years. Height 15in.

Style Informal, mame.
Characteristics Highly scented and fairly floriferous.
Color Creamy white to pale pink flowers in spring.
Care Need to be fed well to encourage flower production. They should be rested each third year. They attract all sorts of insects and fungal diseases and so need regular attention.

MURRAYA SPP.

These are evergreen tropical shrubs originating from China, India and Indonesia. *Murraya paniculata* is the only species used for bonsai and has common names of Satinwood, Orange Jasmine and the Cosmetic Bark Tree. In the West it is grown indoors. They are usually created from cuttings as little material Is found in the wild. They have large glossy leaves and tend to flower throughout the growing season when kept as bonsai.

Style Informal and cascading.
Characteristics Aromatic fragrance.
Color White bell-shaped flowers with red berries in the autumn.
Care Not the easiest of subjects for cultivation. Bright, airy, but draught-free position indoors. Mist regularly, keeping watering to a minimum. Pinch out new growth regularly.

Above. *Murraya paniculata.*
Age 100 years. Height 45in.

NANDINA SPP. SACRED BAMBOO, HEAVENLY BAMBOO

Nandina domestica is the only species in this genus with wide spaced leaflets giving it a bamboo-like appearance. The bark ages quickly giving the young specimens an older look. The flowers are small and white with a hint of yellow and appear in late summer. Several specimens may be placed together in groups, clumps or as a landscape.

Style Informal, upright styles, group plantings, multi-trunked.
Characteristics Heavy trunk and possibly two trunks.
Color Leaves suffused with red before turning green.
Care Bright position and tolerant of light frosts if kept outdoors. Light shade is needed in summer. Indoor plants should be misted daily, even when placed outdoors.

Above. *Nandina domestica.*
Age over 500 years. Height 32in.

PICEA SPP. SPRUCE

Spruce are evergreen conifers. The Norway Spruce (*P. abies*) is familiar as a Christmas tree. The foliage grows on peg-like stumps as needles and branches form in whorls, making it a difficult subject to make into bonsai. Cones are long and hang from the tips of the branches. One of the favored dwarf forms is *P. abies albertiana* 'Conica', which is widely available throughout the world.

Above. *Picea mariana* 'Nan', grown in the mame style.
Age 11 years. Height 4in.

Style Formal, informal, cascading, multi-trunked, mame.
Characteristics Needle foliage and branches which form in whorls.
Color Dark brown, scaly bark.
Care Buds need to be pinched out to just a few needles. Shade from midday sun. Wiring used for training must be applied with the utmost care to avoid killing the branches.

PINUS SPP. PINE

This is the classical bonsai subject in Japan, as they make erect, stately trees, with powerful and tall trunks. Pine foliage is in the form of needles, in bundles of twos or threes. Color varies quite considerably. Japan has an industry producing cheap, quality embryo bonsai material in a host of styles. Restrictions apply to importing pines into Great Britain but European imports, quarantined and certified healthy, can be brought in.

Style Formal, informal, cascading, mame, literati.
Characteristics Powerful and tall trunks often with bark flaking off.
Color Varies quite considerably.
Care Need infrequent potting. Keep needles short by removing buds. Timing is critical. Keep on the dry side and withhold water in spring to restrict needle growth.

Above. Japanese White Pine. Age 30 years. Height 33in.

PODOCARPOS SPP.

This genus resemble the Taxus species (yews), and are often referred to as Yellow Woods or Southern Yews. They are evergreen and have prominent white bands of breathing pores, on the backs of the leaves, called stomata. They are highly prized in the Far East for bonsai, as they are slow-growing. *P.macrophyllus* is the favored subject for bonsai use. Other species used in the West include the dwarf forms *P.nivalis* and *P.alpinus.*

Style Informal or cascading.
Characteristics Horizontal branches and needle-type leaves.
Color Blue-green foliage.
Care Winter protection needed. New growth needs pruning with scissors. Repotting should be undertaken infrequently. Frequent misting is needed indoors and in summer, a long spell outdoors will help keep it healthy.

Above. *Podocarpos macrophyllus.*
Age 60 years. Height 18in.

PRUNUS SPP.

This genus has many different species of flowers and fruit. Leaves are elliptical, and vary in size. The species is known for their fruit—cherries, plums, sloes, damsons, peaches and apricots. As bonsai they are grown for their flowers, which are very showy. Ornamental cherries originate mostly from Japan. There are numerous cultivars found in this genus, the large flowered ones should be avoided for bonsai.

Above. *Prunus pissardii*, Flowering Cherry. Age 8 years. Height 12in.

Style Informal, group planting, mame.
Characteristics Distinctive, deep-colored glossy bark with horizontal breathing cells, known as lenticels.
Color Flowers of pure white through to all shades of pinks or reds.
Care Dead-heading after flowering is needed. Feed only to produce flowers once the basic design of the tree has been created.

PUNICA SPP. POMEGRANATE

They make small, densely twigged deciduous trees with narrow leaves. The dwarf form has better foliage, and is tinged with reds and golds. Few good specimens are found in the West. They can be made by plaiting young trees together or winding around dead material. Large specimens are preferable and will be in proportion to the flowers. *P. granatum* is the species used for bonsai.

Style Informal, multi-trunked, mame, group planting.
Characteristics Powerful and tall trunks often with bark flaking off.
Color Red flowers from mid-summer with light bark.
Care Best kept outdoors in the summer. Need to be given half shade and fed well with fertilizer to encourage flowering. Fruit should not be allowed to grow to full size.

Above. *Punica granatum flaresens.* Age 35 years. Height 20in.

PYRACANTHA SPP. FIRETHORN

An evergreen shrub and quick grower. Small, white hawthorn-like flowers appear in early summer followed by vivid-colored berries in the autumn. They are easily destroyed by frosts when planted in shallow pots. For this reason some consider them indoor bonsai. There are only a few species, the most likely one to be seen is *P. angustifolia*, which is freely flowering and fruiting.

Above. *Pyracantha angustifolia* 'Orange Charmer'. Age 8 years. Height 7in.

Style Informal, cascading, group planting, mame.

Characteristics Brightly colored berries and small Hawthorn-like flowers.

Color Red, orange or yellow berries in the autumn.

Care This is a thirsty species and needs watering even when no growth is taking place. Feed well and rest every third year by removing all the flowers.

PYRUS SPP. PEAR

Pear is an underrated tree, little used for bonsai in Japan or the West. The leaves vary with the species and the bark is rough and deeply furrowed and the tree is characterized by a few erect branches dotted with thorns. The species *P. simonii* is used in Japan, but this is not usually found in the West. The Willow-Leaved Pear (*P. salicifolia*) makes an interesting tree in the weeping style, and the Sand Pear (*P. sinensis*) is well-suited to bonsai.

Above. Pyrus in twin trunk style.
Age 13 years. Height 25in.

Style Informal, multi-trunked, mame, cascading, group plantings.
Characteristics Apple-shaped leaves, rounded rather than long.
Color White strongly scented flowers with crimson centres.
Care They are attacked by a fungus which turns the leaves a deep ebony color. Spraying with fungicide is needed. Dead-head to prevent fruit forming when flowering is over.

P Y R U S

QUERCUS SPP. OAK

Oak is a large genus but not popular as a bonsai subject. The leaves tend to grow in tufts at the end of the twigs which makes them difficult to work with. They also attract many bugs and a whole range of fungal diseases. Most of the species are not suitable for bonsai because of the size of the leaves. They can be deciduous or evergreen but there are few good examples in existence.

Style Formal or informal.
Characteristics Dark gray, fissured bark.
Color Upright, disease-prone, difficult subject.
Care The tendency to attract all kinds of diseases makes this a demanding tree when grown as a bonsai. It does not respond well to pruning and complete defoliation often results in even larger leaves.

Above. English or Truffle Oak.
Age 50 years. Height 33in.

RHODODENDRON SPP. AZELEA, RHODODENDRON

For practical purposes azaleas and rhododendrons are grouped together. They consist of a genus of shrubs renowned for the quality and variety of their flowers. Azaleas are usually used for bonsai as semi-evergreen, rather than deciduous shrubs. They are exclusively confined to the Northern Hemisphere, most species come from China and Tibet.

Style Informal and cascading.
Characteristics Variety and quality of flowers which can obliterate the foliage.
Color Brilliant wide color range.
Care Lime-free soil. Hard water is to be avoided. As bonsai they are not too hardy so winter protection is needed. Frost damage to leaves will cause the tree to regenerate them.

Above. Rhododendron 'Blue Tit'.
Age 30 years. Height 15in.

Above. The flowers of a Satzuki Azelea (*Rhododendron lateritium komei*).

SAGERETIA SPP.

These are small shrubs from Asia, grown as bonsai in China. The branches are stiff and slender and the bark scaly. The leaves are evergreen and have a pinkish tinge when young. Good specimens are being imported but need considerable work to develop their full potential. Those plants from China are said to have been collected from the wild. The species *S. theezans*, for which there is no common name, is almost invariably used as bonsai.

Above. *Sageretia theezans.* Age 100 years. Height 39in.

Style Informal character.
Characteristics Definite masculine appearance with a stiff main stem.
Color White small flowers with a hint of green, developing into small blue berries.
Care They need plenty of light, and can be kept outdoors from late spring to the end of the summer. Needs moderate temperatures all year round and high humidity.

53

SALIX SPP. WILLOW

The Weeping Willow (*S. babylonica*) is the most common member of this genus. The buds on ornamental willows look dead until they start to open and white or pale yellow catkins emerge. The dwarf forms are ideal subjects for bonsai and should have thick and heavy trunks whether the tree is very small or large. For larger-sized bonsai, the White Willow (*S.alba*) and the Weeping Willow (*S. babylonica*) are the best species.

Style Informal, cascading, mame, multi-trunked.
Characteristics Catkin bearing with thick, heavy trunk.
Color Light green foliage, brightly colored red shoots and stems.
Care Thirsty species of tree, and best stood in a bowl of water through the summer. Root growth is vigorous so repotting twice a year is not uncommon. Heavy prune each year to keep foliage compact.

Above. Salix species.
Age 40 years. Height 24in.

Above. Crack Willow *(S. fragilis)*.
Age 12 years. Height 8in.

SERISSA FOETIDA TREE OF A THOUSAND STARS

This is a popular species for indoor bonsai in the West, and as outdoor bonsai in the East. It is an evergreen shrub with small, bright green, oval leaves. Small white flowers cover the tree in late spring. The natural color of the trunk is gray and the bark roughens with age. *S. foetida* is also known as *S. japonica* and is the main species used for bonsai. *Foetida* means foul-smelling, and the bark and roots have a foul smell when cut.

Style Informal, cascading, mame, group plantings, multi-trunked.

Characteristics Slim trunk so a fat trunk will indicate considerable age.

Color White flowers in spring and gray trunk.

Care A subtropical species, *S. foetida* is kept indoors most of the year in a bright position. Regular misting with distilled warm water is appreciated.

Above. *Serrisa foetida.*
Age 15 years. Height 19in.

TAMARIX SPP. TAMARISK

Tamarisks are an ideal subject to use to produce a light and delicate-looking bonsai with slender and graceful branches. The foliage is plume-like and of a light green color. In mid-spring they produce light-pink flowers. The arching branches will give a weeping style. Tamarisks belong to a genus with only a few species and even fewer varieties and cultivars. Two of the common species are *T. juniperiana* and *T. pentandra*.

Style Formal or informal.
Characteristics Plume-like foliage.
Color Small white flowers in the spring.
Care Not easy to cultivate, Tamarisks can die for no known reason. Pruning has to be carried out at the correct time as some flower on old wood. Full sunlight is usually required.

Above. *Tamarix chinensis.*
Age 30 years. Height 14in.

Above. *Taxus baccata.*
Age 15 years. Extent 20in from apex to tail.

TAXUS SPP. YEW

Yews make high quality bonsai but there are few good specimens in the West. The needles are arranged spirally around the shoot and appear as though in two flattened ranks. At first, trees grow erect but spread with age. Trunks are slim, and heavy trunks on old trees are thought to be not one trunk but a fusion of several. The bark is purple and scaly. When in flower they shed an enormous amount of fine, creamy white pollen.

Style Informal, cascading, literati, group plantings, multi-trunked.
Characteristics Needles are arranged spirally around the shoots. Scaly bark.
Color Bark is purple-red.
Care Easy to maintain. Pluck out the ends of new growth to maintain the shape. Happy in heavy shade. A female tree is needed to produce fruit. Yews grown from seed are usually male**.**

Above. *Taxus baccata.*
Age 12 years. Height 11in.

TSUGA SPP. HEMLOCK

Hemlocks look similar to firs but are more delicately foliaged and have smaller leaves. The branches droop naturally and the cones are small and pale brown when mature. The Eastern or Canadian Hemlock (*T. canadensis*) is available in a range of varieties, most are shrubby and very appealing as bonsai. Dwarf forms are more likely to be used as they are available from garden centers.

Style Formal, informal, cascading.
Characteristics Delicately foliaged with small leaves.
Color Cinnamon-red bark, deeply furrowed with age.
Care Grow slowly and new growth is the same color as the old foliage so the tree can get out of shape. Shade is needed for the summer.

Above. *Tsuga canadensis* 'Jedolah'. Age 20 years. Height 15in.

T S U G A

ULMUS SPP. ELM

Elms, until Dutch Elm Disease, were a major feature of the countryside and the suburbs. Now only a few remain. They have a distinctive deciduous leaves, which are offset slightly. Few elm bonsai are seen, as little suitable material is available. One cultivar which is recommended is the hybrid *U. elegantissima* 'Jacqueline Hillier', a tree bearing small leaves and compact foliage.

Style Formal, informal, cascading, mame, group plantings.
Characteristics Tall, narrow, erect trees with sucker growth from the base.
Color Thick, deeply furrowed brown bark.
Care Many elms sucker freely, in bonsai this must be removed. Wind and sun protection is necessary. Bonsai specimens do not get attacked by Dutch Elm Disease.

Above. English Elm.
Age 30 years. Height 42in.

WISTERIA SPP.

Wisteria are actually vines and grow up the sides of walls. This is a classic flowering bonsai subject of impressive quality when well designed. Many low quality wisteria bonsai are imported from Japan and do not conform to the usual bonsai style as they need to show off the long racemes of flowers up to 1ft long. Few species exist of this climber. Japanese Wisteria (*W. floribunda*) or Chinese Wisteria (*W. sinensis*) are both used for bonsai.

Style Informal or cascading.
Characteristics Pronounced slope to the trunk and unique flowers.
Color Flowers range from white to shades of blue, purple and pink.
Care A quick grower, needs a lot of attention to keep it under control. Flowering is difficult to achieve. Fertilizers low in nitrogen should be applied to encourage flower production.

Above. Chinese Wisteria. Age 12 years. Height 14in.

  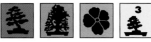

ZELKOVA SPP.

Only in recent times have zelkovas been used for bonsai, and now imported plants are often available in bonsai nurseries. They make massive deciduous trees with powerful trunks and are confused with elms because the leaves are similar. Autumn color is good and is enhanced through defoliation. They only have a few species, and normally the Saw-Leaved or Japanese Zelkova (*Z. serrata*) is used for bonsai.

Above. *Zelkova serrata.*
Age 45 years. Height 31in.

Style Informal, literati, group plantings, multi-trunked.
Characteristics Powerful trunks with interesting bark.
Color Bronze, orange and red in autumn.
Care Defoliation, by hand, is carried out in the year it is repotted, to keep leaves small.

Index